MW00596758

Silences in NGO discourse:
The role and future of
NGOs in Africa

Fahamu Books

Patrick Burnett & Firoze Manji (eds) (2007) *From the Slave Trade to 'Free' Trade: How Trade Undermines Democracy and Justice in Africa*. Oxford: Fahamu. ISBN: 978-0-9545637-1-4

Issa G. Shivji (2007) *Silences in NGO Discourse: The Role and Future of NGOs in Africa*. Oxford: Fahamu. ISBN: 978-0-9545637-5-2

Firoze Manji & Stephen Marks (eds) (2007) *African Perspectives on China in Africa*. Nairobi and Oxford: Fahamu. ISBN: 978-0-9545637-3-8

Patrick Burnett, Shereen Karmali & Firoze Manji (eds) (2007) *Grace, Tenacity and Eloquence: The Struggle for Women's Rights in Africa*. Nairobi and Oxford: Fahamu & Solidarity for African Women's Rights (SOAWR). ISBN: 978-0-9545637-2-1

Roselynn Musa, Faiza Jama Mohammed & Firoze Manji (eds) (2006) *Breathing Life into the African Union Protocol on Women's Rights in Africa*. Oxford, Nairobi & Addis Ababa: Fahamu, SOAWR & the African Union Commission Directorate of Women, Gender and Development. ISBN: 978-1-904855-66-8

Roselynn Musa, Faiza Jama Mohammed & Firoze Manji (eds) (2006) *Vulgarisation du protocole de l'union africaine sur les droits des femmes en Afrique*. Oxford, Nairobi & Addis Ababa: Fahamu, SOAWR & the African Union Commission Directorate of Women, Gender and Development. ISBN: 978-1-904855-68-2

Firoze Manji & Patrick Burnett (eds) (2005) *African Voices on Development and Social Justice: Editorials from Pambazuka News 2004*. Dar es Salaam: Mkuki na Nyota Publishers. ISBN: 978-9987-417-35-3

SILENCES IN NGO DISCOURSE:
THE ROLE AND FUTURE OF
NGOS IN AFRICA

ISSA G. SHIVJI

PAMBAZUKA

First published 2007 by Fahamu – Networks for Social Justice
Nairobi & Oxford
www.fahamu.org
www.pambazuka.org

Fahamu, 2nd floor, 51 Cornmarket Street, Oxford OX1 3HA, UK

Fahamu Kenya, PO Box 47158, 00100 GPO, Nairobi, Kenya

Copyright © 2007 Issa G. Shivji

All rights reserved. No part of this publication may be reproduced or
transmitted in any form or by any other means without the written
permission of the copyright holder, except in accordance with the
provisions of the Copyright Act 1956 (as amended). Application for the
copyright holders' written permission to reproduce or transmit any part
of this publication should be addressed to the publishers.

British Library Cataloguing in Publication Data
A catalogue record for this book is available from the British Library

ISBN: 978-0-9545637-5-2

Cover illustration and design by Judith Charlton, Fahamu
Manufactured on demand by Lightning Source

Contents

Publisher's foreword
Firoze Manji   vii

About Pambazuka News   xi

About Fahamu   xii

About the author   xiii

Part 1
Silences in NGO discourse:
The role and future of NGOs in Africa   1

Part 2
Reflections on NGOs in Tanzania:
What we are, what we are not and what
we ought to be   53

...the transformation from a colonial subject society to a bourgeois society in Africa is incomplete, stunted and distorted. We have the continued domination of imperialism – reproduction of the colonial mode – in a different form, currently labelled globalisation or neoliberalism. Within this context, NGOs are neither a third sector, nor independent of the state. Rather, they are inextricably imbricated in the neoliberal offensive, which follows on the heels of the crisis of the national project. Unless there is awareness on the part of the NGOs of this fundamental moment in the struggle between imperialism and nationalism, they end up playing the role of ideological and organisational foot soldiers of imperialism...

Issa G. Shivji

Publisher's foreword

Aid, in which NGOs play a significant role, is frequently portrayed as a form of altruism, a charitable act that enables wealth to flow from rich to poor, poverty to be reduced and the poor empowered. Such claims tend to be, as David Sogge puts it 'shibboleths, catch phrases that distinguish believers from doubters. Indeed they are utterances of belief. At best they are half-truths'.[1]

The market and voluntarism have a long association; the first and most celebrated period of 'free trade', from the 1840s to the 1930s, was also a high point of charitable activity throughout the British empire. In Britain itself, the industrial revolution opened up a great gulf between the bourgeoisie and the swelling ranks of the urban proletariat. In the 1890s, when industrialists were amassing fortunes to rival those of the aristocracy, as much as a third of the population of London was living below the level of bare subsistence. Death from starvation was not unknown. At this time, private philanthropy was the preferred solution to social need, and private expenditure far outweighed public provision.

It is hardly surprising that in the current era of neoliberalism we are seeing, once again, a flourishing of NGOs: the new missionaries to Africa. While such institutions had some presence in Africa in the post second world war period, it was really only in the 1980s and 1990s, as structural adjustment programmes were imposed across Africa by the international financial institutions and development agencies, that NGOs really flourished, gradually taking over the work of the retrenching state that had been persuaded to disengage from the provision of social services to its populations. The bilateral and multilateral institutions set aside significant funds aimed at 'mitigating' the 'social dimensions of adjustment'. The purpose of such programmes was to be palliatives that would minimise the more glaring inequalities perpetuated by their policies. Funds were made available to ensure that a so-called 'safety net' of social services would be provided for the 'vulnerable' – but this time not by the state (which had after all been forced to 'retrench' away from the social sector) but by the ever-willing NGO sector.

The possession of such funds was to have a profound impact on the very nature of the NGO sector. This was a period in which the involvement of Northern NGOs in Africa grew dramatically. In the ten years between 1984 and 1994, the British government increased its funding to NGOs by almost 400 per cent, to £68,700,000. NGOs in Australia, Finland, Norway and Sweden all saw similar increases in official funding from the early 1980s onwards. As a consequence of the increased levels of funding and increased attention, the number of development organisations in Western countries mushroomed, and many established NGOs experienced spectacular growth.

Over the last two decades, development NGOs have become an integral, and necessary, part of a system that sacrifices respect for justice and rights. They have taken what has been described elsewhere as the 'missionary position' – delivering services, running projects that are motivated by charity and pity, and doing things for people (who, implicitly, cannot do them for themselves), albeit dressed up with the verbiage of participatory approaches.[2]

It would be wrong to present the relationship between Western NGOs and official aid agencies in the 1980s as the product of some conscious conspiracy, as was clearly the case with colonial missionary organisations. The precondition for the co-option of NGOs into the neoliberal cause merely reflects a coincidence in ideologies, rather than a purposeful plan. The proponents of neoliberalism saw in charitable development the possibility of enforcing the unjust social order they desired by consensual rather than coercive means.

The role NGOs have played in expanding and consolidating neoliberal hegemony in the global context may have been unwitting. It may not have been as direct or as underhand as some of the activities willingly taken up by colonial missionary societies and voluntary organisations. But that is not to say it is any less significant. Indeed, one could argue that it has actually been more effective.

Because many NGOs do provide much needed services, because their motives are often honourable, because they employ capable and often progressive staff, there has been a reluctance amongst many to discuss critically the objective impact of their work as distinct from the subjective motives behind their work.

Issa Shivji has long been one of the most articulate critics of the destructive effects of neoliberal policies in Africa, in particular of the ways in which the gains of independence have been eroded, not merely at the behest of imperial powers, but also with the willing collusion of the local comprador class. His regular essays in the Tanzania press have been a beacon for those of us who grapple with understanding the post-independence onslaught on our countries that has led to a norm whereby it is accepted that social and economic policies should be determined not by the electorate, but rather by a small elite that seeks its legitimacy (and power) from London, Washington, Berlin and Paris.

The two essays in this book have appeared in abridged form elsewhere. But because of the importance of the subject, and because the richness of the arguments presented by Shivji need to be heard in full, we are pleased to be able to make them available to a wider audience.

Firoze Manji is editor of Pambazuka News and director of Fahamu.

Notes

1 David Sogge (2002) *Give and Take: what's the matter with foreign aid.* London: Zed Books.

2 Firoze Manji and Carl O'Coill (2002) 'The missionary position: NGOs and development in Africa', *International Affairs*, 78(3): p. 567–83.

About Pambazuka News

Pambazuka News is the authoritative pan-African news-letter and platform for social justice in Africa, offering comprehensive weekly coverage, cutting edge commentary and in-depth analysis on politics and current affairs, development, human rights, refugees, gender issues and culture in Africa. It is intended as a tool for progressive social change.

Published by Fahamu, Pambazuka News is produced by a pan-African community of some 300 writers and contributor – academics, social activists, women's organisations, social movements, civil society organisations, artists, poets, bloggers and commentators. Since its establishment in 2000, more than 300 issues in English and French have been published, representing some of the most important analyses of current affairs in Africa.

Some 40,000 articles, analyses and news items have been published and stored for free access on an online database, disseminated by email and news feeds, reproduced on numerous websites, and distributed in print form at numerous forums, including African Union summits. Pambazuka News currently has an estimated audience of half a million readers.

You can subscribe to Pambazuka News at www.pambazuka.org or send an email to editor@pambazuka.org with the word 'subscribe' in the subject line.

About Fahamu

Fahamu (www.fahamu.org) has a vision of the world where people organise to emancipate themselves from all forms of oppression, recognise their social responsibilities, respect each other's differences, and realise their full potential.

Fahamu supports the struggle for human rights and social justice in Africa through the innovative use of information and communication technologies; stimulating debate, discussion and analysis; distributing news and information; developing training materials and running distance-learning courses. Fahamu focuses primarily on Africa, although we work with others to support the global movement for human rights and social justice. The word 'Fahamu' means 'understanding' or 'consciousness' in Kiswahili.

About the author

Issa G. Shivji is one of Africa's most radical and original thinkers. A public intellectual, he remains amongst Africa's leading experts on law and development issues. He has served as an advocate of the high court and the Court of Appeal of Tanzania since 1977, and as an advocate of the high court in Zanzibar since 1989.

Shivji has recently retired from his formal position as professor of law at the University of Dar es Salaam, Tanzania where he has taught since 1970. He has taught and worked in universities all over the world, including the University of Zimbabwe, the University of Warwick, the University of Hong Kong and el Colegio de Mexico.

He is a prolific writer and researcher, producing over a dozen books, monographs and articles, as well as a weekly column published in national newspapers.

His books include the seminal *Concept of Human Rights in Africa* (CODESRIA, 1989); *Class Struggles in Tanzania* (Tanzania Publishing House, 1976); *The State and the Working People in Tanzania* (CODESRIA, 1986), *Not Yet Democracy: Reforming Land Tenure in Tanzania* (IIED, 1998), and *Let the People Speak: Tanzania Down the Road to Neoliberalism* (CODESRIA, 2006). He co-edited *Constitutional and Legal System of Tanzania: A Civics Sourcebook* (Mkuki na Nyota Publishers, 2004).

He has contributed some 15 articles to Pambazuka News.

SILENCES IN NGO DISCOURSE: THE ROLE AND FUTURE OF NGOS IN AFRICA₁

Preface

This paper examines critically the role and future of the NGO in Africa in the light of its self-perception as a non-governmental, non-political, non-partisan, non-ideological, non-academic, non-theoretical, non-profit association of well-intentioned individuals dedicated to changing the world to make it a better place for the poor, marginalised and downcast. The paper argues that the role of NGOs in Africa cannot be understood without clear characterisation of the current historical moment.

On a canvass of broad strokes, I depict Africa at the crossroads of the defeat of the national project and the rehabilitation of the imperial project. Faced with an avalanche of diatribe about the 'end of history', I find it necessary, albeit briefly, to reiterate the history of Africa's enslavement: from the first contacts with the Europeans five centuries ago, through the slave trade, to colonialism, and now globalisation. The aim of this historical detour is to demonstrate the fundamental antithesis between the national and the imperial projects, so as to identify correctly the place and role of NGOs within them.

1

 SILENCES IN NGO DISCOURSE

I locate the rise, prominence and privileging of the NGO sector in the womb of the neoliberal offensive. Its aims are ideological, economic and political. I argue that NGO discourse, or more correctly, non-discourse, is predicated on the philosophical and political premises of the neoliberal or globalisation paradigm. It is in this context that I will discuss the 'five silences', or blind spots, in NGO discourse. I then draw out the implications of these silences for the contemporary and future roles of the NGO sector in Africa.

Before I begin, I must make two confessions. First, my paper is undoubtedly critical, sometimes ruthlessly so, but not cynical. Second, this criticism is also self-criticism, since the author has been involved in NGO activism for some 15 years. Finally, I must make clear that I do not doubt the noble motivations and good intentions of NGO leaders and activists. But we do not judge the outcome of a process by the intentions of its authors. We aim to analyse the objective effects of actions, regardless of their intentions.

The national project and its impediments

1885: The slicing of the African cake

By 1885, when European kings, princes and presidents sat in Berlin to slice up the African continent with their geometrical instruments, the African people had already been devastated by the ravages of the West Atlantic slave trade. In West and Central Africa, the indigenous civilisations lay in ruins, from the sophisticated Saharan trade routes with Timbuktu at their centre, to the empires of Angola (Davidson 1961). On the Eastern seaboard, the European invasion, led by the Portuguese, defeated and destroyed the city states of Swahili civilisation (Davidson 1961) (Sheriff 1987). All in all, some 40,000,000 souls are estimated to have perished in the triangular slave trade, which lasted for roughly four centuries, 1450–1850.

The development of the European and North American industrial revolution and the global lead this gave to Europe and America was in no small measure built on the back of Africans (Williams 1945). The colonial episode was thus the tail end of long and destructive contact between Europe and Africa. The slave trade tore apart the very social fabric of African societies, destroying their internal processes of change. It imposed on the continent a European worldview in which the peoples of Africa were at the lowest rung of the so-called civilised order. No other continent, including those that suffered formal European colonisation, had their social, cultural and moral order destroyed on this scale.

Dominant European historiography recounts at best the colonial episode, while ignoring four centuries of precolonial contact. Yet the present cannot be fully understood and grasped, nor the future charted, without constantly keeping in the forefront of our minds the century-old processes cited by Walter Rodney as 'how Europe underdeveloped Africa' (Rodney 1972).

The precolonial and colonial legacy of Africa is a continuing saga of domination, exploitation and humiliation of the continent by European and American imperial powers. My thesis is that this imperial relationship continues, notwithstanding a brief period of nationalism. Below, I briefly recapitulate the salient features of the colonial legacy and the abortive national project.

3

 SILENCES IN NGO DISCOURSE

The colonial legacy

Right from inception, the most important feature of colonialism was the division of the continent into countries and states cutting across 'natural' geographic, cultural ethnic and economic ties that had evolved historically. The consequences were thus.

Boundaries were artificially drawn, with rulers literally reflecting the balance of strength and power among the imperial states. The boundaries divided up peoples, cultures, natural resources and historical affinities. Moreover, these newly created countries became subjects of different European powers with their own traditions of political rule, public administration, cultural outlooks, languages and systems of education. Africa was never Africa: it was Anglo-phone, Franco-phone, or Luso-phone.

Colonial economies answering to the needs and exigencies of metropolitan powers were disintegrated and disarticulated. Notorious export-oriented, vertically-integrated economies based on raw materials exports and the import of manufactured goods were the result. Internal processes of specialisation and division of labour with mutual interdependence – craftsmen and cultivators, producers and merchants, industry and agriculture – as possible harbingers of future industrial development were deliberately destroyed and systematically discouraged (Kjekshus 1977, 1996). Within and between countries, development was extremely uneven.

Of course the underlying economic logic of the colonial economy was the exploitation of natural and human resources. Colonies became sites for generating surplus while the metropoles were sites of accumulation. The result was the development of the centres and the under-development of the peripheries. Production processes relied heavily on coercion rather than on contractual consensus for reproduction: forced labour, forced peasant production, enforced cash-crop sales, restrictions on organisation and association and the criminalisation of 'civil relations'. For example, the breach of employment

---

I do not doubt the noble motivations and good intentions of NGO leaders and activists. But we do not judge the outcome of a process by the intentions of its authors. We aim to analyse the objective effects of actions, regardless of their intentions.

---

contracts led to penal sanctions, as did the non-cultivation of minimum acreages of cash and food crops. Thus force was integrated into the process of production (Mamdani 1987) (Shivji 1987, 1998).

People were divided along ethnic, religious and racial lines. Some tribes were labelled martial, therefore a recruiting ground for soldiers. Others were condemned to be labourers and their areas became labour reservoirs. Others were supposed to provide political henchmen for the colonial state apparatus. Missionary education became

the means by which Christianity would be spread and the souls of pagans saved, whilst producing the future educated elite. Indigenous religions and worldviews were condemned as pagan. There was systematic discrimination against Islam, one of the oldest religions to enter and be internalised in Africa.

Existing internal social divisions and stratification of African society were condemned. Africans were condemned as lazy and indolent, incapable of learning and entrepreneurship. They were to be perpetually ruled and disciplined, suppressed and muted. Meanwhile traders, craftsmen and skilled labour were imported: South Asians into East Africa, Lebanese into West Africa. Thus a hierarchy of racial privilege was constructed, the epitome of which was the settler colony. The middle classes that developed in the interstices of the colonised social order were at best stunted, at worst caricatures (Fanon 1963).

Religion and education became vehicles for reproducing colonial racial and cultural complexes: white as superior, black as inferior. The white man's beliefs were 'a religion'. The black man's were 'witchcraft' or 'black magic'. The white man's means of communication was language; the black man's was dialect. As Fanon (1963, p. 32) put it:

> The native is declared insensible to ethics; he represents not only the absence of values, but also the negation of values. ... The customs of the colonized people, their traditions, their myths – above all, their myths – are the very sign of that poverty of spirit and of their constitutional depravity. ... The Church in the colonies is the white people's Church, the foreigner's

Church. She does not call the native to God's ways but to the ways of the white man, of the master, of the oppressor. And as we know, in this matter many are called but few chosen.

The 'few chosen', the colonised elite, were thus a caricature, alienated from their own people, yet not fully accepted by their master. Sartre (1963, p. 7) sums it up well in his preface to Fanon:

The European élite undertook to manufacture a native élite. They picked out promising adolescents; they branded them, as with a red-hot iron, with the principles of western culture; they stuffed their mouths full with high-sounding phrases, grand glutinous words that stuck to the teeth. After a short stay in the mother country they were sent home, whitewashed. These walking lies had nothing left to say to their brothers; they only echoed. From Paris, from London, from Amsterdam we would utter words 'Parthenon! Brotherhood!' and somewhere in Africa or Asia lips would open '...thenon! ...therhood!' It was the golden age.

The colonial state was an implant, an alien apparatus imposed on the colonised society. It was an excrescence of the metropolitan state without the latter's liberal institutions or politics. It was a despotic state. In the colonial social formation, it did not have its own civil society. So-called civil society was effectively the metropolitan civil society, at best, the narrow European settler community in

7

the colony. The colonised society was a subject-society, a collection of 'heathens' or 'natives', governed by coercion, regulated by custom. It was not a civil society, constituted by citizens, governed by rights and duties, regulated by law (Mamdani 1996).

The governance structures of the colonial state reflected and reinforced the racial, ethnic and religious divisions and fragmentations of the colonised society. For the subject society, the policeman, the tax collector and the district commissioner doubling up as a magistrate represented the state, not the legislative councillor or judge. To resolve a dispute with a neighbour, the 'native' went to a chief. To be punished for murder, or non-payment of tax, or theft of a master's property, he was dragged to the magistrate or judge to be imprisoned or hanged.

We may sum up then by stating the obvious. On the eve of independence, African nationalists faced the formidable task of transforming brutalised colonial societies into national societies. The national project thus called for an African revolution in every sense of the word.

The nationalist challenge and the defeat of the national project

The first challenge and defeat: Pan-Africanism versus territorial nationalism

Colonial divisiveness, both within and between African countries, seriously undermined the national project from inception. The colonial infrastructure was the exact antithesis of a national economy. The only rationale behind individual African countries as loci of national independence was the fact that each one of them fell under the jurisdiction of a different colonial power. In sum, the colonial rationale became the rationale of the national project: a contradiction in terms and a paradox.

This paradox was acutely felt, if not always clearly understood, by first generation African nationalists. Tutored in the ways of their European counterparts, African nationalists coined and crafted the demands of their peoples in the European idiom of human rights and national self-determination within an international context which had witnessed a rise of national liberation in the post-war period. Yet, the ideological genesis of African nationalism lay in pan-Africanism. The locus of pan-Africanism was the continent itself, not the artificially created spaces bound by colonial borders called countries.

Literally, therefore, pan-Africanism begat nationalism, rather than the other way round. Pan-Africanism preceded nationalism by almost half a century. Logic and history neatly coincided. The founding fathers of pan-Africanism were African-Americans, the African diaspora, whose identity could only be African, and not Nigerian or Congolese or Kenyan. The leading lights of the independence movement – Kwame Nkrumah, Jomo Kenyatta – were incubated, conceived, propagated and organised in the pan-African movement by the likes of the great George Padmore, W. E. B. DuBois and C. L. R. James (Legum 1965).

When Nkrumah returned to the continent, his vision was of a West African federation, rather than an independent Gold Coast. At the threshold of Ghana's indepen-

9

dence, Nkrumah, with great foresight, undertook such historical initiatives as the All Africa People's Conferences, bringing together independence parties and trade unions. Leading African nationalists including Nyerere realised and repeated on many occasions that there could be no African nationalism without pan-Africanism: 'African nationalism is meaningless, is anachronistic, and is dangerous, if it is not at the same time Pan-Africanism' (Nyerere 1963, 1967). Nyerere was even prepared to delay the independence of his country in order to facilitate the East African federation. He argued that once these countries became independent, with their own flags, national anthems, presidents and prime ministers, it would be much more difficult to dis-solve individual sovereignties into a larger sovereignty. History proved him right.

Nkrumah constantly and vehemently argued that left on their own, independent African countries would become pawns on the imperialist chessboard. He too was tragically proved right in the case of the Congo. Under the guise of the United Nations, led by the United States, Western imperial powers conspired in the assassination of the great nationalist leader Patrice Lumumba, perpetuating Congo's descent into a cycle of violence, from which it has yet to recover.

As one after another African countries became indepen-dent, Nkrumah's All Africa Peoples Conferences dissolved into the Conferences of Independent African States, which eventually formed the Organisation of African Unity (OAU). To the chagrin even of his own friends, Nkrumah continued his battle cry for a union of African states.

Nyerere advocated a gradualist-cum-regional approach

to African unity. He clashed with Nkrumah, who believed that the regional approach to African unity would in fact become an obstacle to political unity of the continent, and that regionalism would inevitably play into the hands of imperialism (Shivji 2005). Logic was on the side of Nyerere, but history and political economy proved Nkrumah right.

With great foresight, Nkrumah wrote *Neo-Colonialism, the Last Stage of Imperialism*, for which imperialism never forgave him. He was overthrown in 1966 by a CIA-sponsored coup. Nyerere's own practical attempt to unite Zanzibar with Tanganyika in 1964 can more accurately be considered a pragmatic response to intense cold war pressures than an example of pan-African unity (Wilson 1989). The OAU itself was bedeviled by imperial machinations, which led to Nyerere, one of its founding fathers, angrily condemning it as a 'trade union of African leaders/states'.

The national project inevitably and inexorably became a statist project. Nationalism resolved itself into various ideologies of developmentalism and nation-building. In the process, it undermined pan-Africanism (Shivji 1986) (Wamba 1991, 1996). Ironically, territorial nationalism became the gravedigger of pan-Africanism, out of which it was born. While paying full tribute to Nkrumah's great vision at the 40th anniversary of Ghana's independence in 1997, Nyerere (1997) lamented the failure of first generation nationalists to unite Africa:

Once you multiply national anthems, national flags and national passports, seats at the United Nations, and individuals entitled to 21 guns salute, not to speak of a host of ministers, Prime ministers, and

11

 SILENCES IN NGO DISCOURSE

envoys, you would have a whole army of powerful people with vested interests in keeping Africa
balkanized.

The second challenge and defeat:
the developmental state versus democratic
development

The independence movement in Africa was essentially
led by the proto-middle classes, or petty bourgeoisie,
consisting mostly of the educated elite. No doubt it was a
mass movement in which Africans were reasserting their
Africanness after five centuries of domination and humiliation. Tom Mboya called it 'the rediscovery of Africa by
Africans' (Mboya 1963). Amilcar Cabral defined national
liberation as the process of 'becoming Africans' (Cabral
1980). Yet, as some African nationalists had predicted and
others painfully realised, territorial nationalism turned
out to be an anachronism.

African nationalists including Nyerere, who took the
reins of state at the dawn of independence, had to work
within the constraints imposed by territorial nationalism. In
the process, they ended up making virtue of necessity, and
the authoritarian logic of the colonial state was reasserted.

The independent state, as Nyerere argued, had the twin
tasks of development and nation-building. It preceded
the nation (Nyerere 1963). Ironically however, the state
that was supposed to build the nation had inherited the
colonial state: it was despotic and divisive, in every respect
antithetical to the tasks of nation-building. Nationalism
in the hands of the post-colonial state degenerated into

statism: politically authoritarian, economically rapacious, internationally compradorial and nationally dictatorial. At best, the ideology of nationalism resolved into various ideologies of developmentalism; at worst it became ethnicism. The liberal constitutional order that the depart-

---

NGO discourse, or more correctly, non-discourse, is predicated on the philosophical and political premises of the neoliberal or globalisation paradigm.

---

ing colonial masters bequeathed was a tragic joke, because it was superimposed on a despotic apparatus, which had been invented, strengthened and bequeathed by the colonial master. The despotic infrastructure endured while the liberal superstructure blew off into the winds of factional political struggles, or so-called development imperatives (Shivji 2003).

'We must run while others walk', Nyerere declared. In the hurry to develop, he added, 'we cannot afford liberal checks and balances'. Justifying the executive or 'imperial' presidency, as it is branded in African jurisprudence, Nyerere wrote in the (London) *Observer* (Mwaikusa 1995, p. 105):

Our constitution differs from the American system in that it ... enables the executive to function without being checked at every turn .... Our need is not for

13

 SILENCES IN NGO DISCOURSE

brakes to social change ... – our lack of trained man-
power and capital resources, and even our climate,
act too effectively already. We need accelerators
powerful enough to overcome the inertia bred by
poverty, and the resistances which are inherent in all
societies.

Independence had raised expectations. To maintain legitimacy, the new regimes had to deliver on both developmental and social fronts. But the colonial state had deliberately
suppressed and undermined the development of a middle
class, which would have become an agency for development. So it fell to the state. Regardless of the variety of the
ideology, whether capitalist or nominally socialist, the state
became a site of private and public accumulation. The public sector played the dominant role in all African countries,
from socialist Tanzania to capitalist Malawi. Nyerere justified his programme of nationalisation more on the grounds
of economic nationalism than on the principles of socialism
(Nyerere 1968). Whatever the pundits of neoliberalism may
proclaim today, the fact remains that the Bretton Woods
institutions, together with the so-called 'donor community'
and the multinationals, used the African state to serve its
own interest while turning a blind eye to mismanagement
and corruption.

During the first decade and a half of independence,
African economies showed modest growth rates in compar-
ison to other continents. Nonetheless, they were impressive
given the conditions imposed at independence. Investment
and savings ranged between 15-20 per cent of GDP.
Primary and secondary school enrolment was expanded.

Tertiary education, which in many countries literally did not exist during colonial times, was introduced. Medical and health statistics showed improvement. But this growth and development were unsustainable, as they were predicated on the reinforcement of colonial foundations.

Growth in agriculture production was based on extensive cultivation rather than a rise in productivity using the industrial processes of fertilisation, mechanisation and irrigation. It depended heavily on exports of a few primary commodities traded on a hostile and adverse international market. Growth in the manufacturing sector was heavily dependent on import-substitution and intermediary inputs, with few internal linkages. Investment was largely public, while private domestic capital was stashed away in foreign countries. According to one estimate, by 1990, 37 per cent of Africa's wealth had flown outside the continent (Mkandawire & Soludo 1999). Moreover, foreign capital concentrated in the extractive industries simply hemorrhaged the economy, rather than contributing to its development.

During this period, the developmental state also borrowed heavily, whether for genuinely productive or prestige projects. Petro-dollars accumulated by international banks during the 1973 oil crisis were offloaded in the form of cheap loans to developing countries. But by the end of 1970s, cheap loans had turned into heavy debt burdens as the limits of the early growth were reached. The economic shocks of the late 1970s plunged African economies further into deep crisis. Numbers fell, growth rates became negative, debt repayments became unsustainable, fiscal imbalances and inflation were out of control. Social services

declined, infrastructure deteriorated. One after another, African governments – including the radical nationalists – found themselves pleading at the door of the IMF and the Paris club (Campbell & Stein).

Economists have described the 1980s as Africa's lost decade. The 1980s were also a transition period marking the beginnings of the decline of developmentalism and the rise of neoliberalism, euphemistically called globalisation. The lost decade signalled both the decline of the developmental state and the loss of its political legitimacy: the loss of both development and democracy. Internally, political stirrings and rethinking began, both practical and ideological.

But as the African political economy has again and again demonstrated, the continent is firmly inserted in the imperialist web. Instead of allowing a space to open up for internal popular struggles, the opportunist imperialist intervention derailed it by imposing top-down, so-called multi-party democracy and 'good governance'. Western powers took the opportunity to reassert their political and ideological hegemony. They recovered the ground lost during the nationalist decades, a trajectory worth recapitulating.

The third challenge and defeat: nationalism versus imperialism

Colonialism left by the front door and returned through the back door in the form of neocolonialism. Radical nationalists such as Nkrumah and Ben Bella were overthrown in military coups. Lumumba, Pio Gama Pinto and Thomas Sankara were assassinated in Western sponsored imperial adventures (Blum 1986, 2001) (De Witte 2001). The few who survived including Nyerere and Kaunda did so through compromise and a game of hide-and-seek. Others, for example Sékou Touré, became paranoid and despotic, apprehensive of being overthrown or assassinated. Others – Kenyatta, Moi, Houphet Boigny and Senghor – simply became compradors in the bidding of their imperial masters.

Reiterating the need to build nations out of fractious ethnic groups and for rapid development, the post-independence ruling classes and governing elites centralised and concentrated power in the executive arm of the state. On the other hand, they hegemonised autonomous expressions of civil society (Shivji 1991). Elsewhere, ruling factions resorted to whipping up ethnic divisions to retain power.

Yet, it is also true that during this period, imperialism was ideologically on the defensive. The movement of the newly independent countries, principles of non-alignment, UNCTAD, the 'new economic world order', the right to development, the successful Chinese, Cuban, and Nicaraguan revolutions, the defeat of the US in Vietnam, and the worldwide student anti-imperialist movement enhanced the prestige of national liberation movements. This was a period labelled by Samir Amin as 'the period of Bandung excitement' (Amin 1990).

For Africa generally, the triumph of the armed struggles in Mozambique, Angola and Guinea Bissau represented ironically enough both the high point of radical nationalism and its precipitous decline in the next decade. Portugal was the weak link in the imperialist chain. It was defeated

17

 SILENCES IN NGO DISCOURSE

by the national liberation movement supported by much of the rest of Africa.

But imperialism was not destroyed. The national liberation movement in power had embarked on an alternative, anti-imperialist development path. The struggle between nationalism and imperialism found its most concentrated expression in southern Africa. Imperialism, through its proxy, apartheid South Africa, showed its true colours by supporting terrorist organisations: RENAMO

...the present cannot be fully understood and grasped, nor the future charted, without constantly keeping in the forefront of our minds the century-old processes cited by Walter Rodney as 'how Europe underdeveloped Africa'.

---

in Mozambique and UNITA in Angola. Such organisations caused havoc leading to compromises on all fronts, change in direction of development and loss of the national liberation vision. The national liberation elites became utterly beholden, disowning their own past, slavishly echoing rising neoliberal rhetoric.

As history will have it, the quasi success of the South African national liberation movement, one of the longest standing and most militant, was not the high point in the stand of radical nationalism against imperialism, rather the beginning of its end. By the end of the 1970s and early

1980s, the nationalist era, particularly its territorial variant, was drawing to a close. The defeat of socialism in Eastern Europe and the Soviet Union further narrowed the space for the expression of radical nationalism and anti-imperialism.

Imperialism took the offensive, initially on the economic front with its structural adjustment programmes. This was soon followed by an undisguised political and ideological offensive, ridiculing and humiliating nationalism, while rehabilitating imperialism. In 1990 Douglas Hurd, the then British foreign secretary, was able to say: 'we are slowly putting behind us a period of history in which the West was unable to express a legitimate interest in the developing world without being accused of "neo-colonialism"' (Furedi 1994). The British historian, John Charmley, launching his book *Churchill: The End of Glory* (p. 98) could unashamedly declare:

> The British Empire vanishing has had a very deleterious effect on the third world. Look at Uganda under the British and look at it now. And you didn't get famines quite as frequently in Africa then as you do now.

The neoliberal package is and has been more an ideological offensive than simply an economic programme. But let us not jump ahead. Instead I shall retrace the beginnings of the neoliberal phase in Africa.

The imperial project and its succours

The neoliberal offensive

The imperialist offensive came on the heel of the defeat of the national project to destroy and bury it. This was, by definition, the immanent dream of imperialism. On the economic front, the neoliberal package boils down to further deepening the integration of African economies in the world capitalist system, thus reproducing essentially colonial and neocolonial economic structures.

In 1981 the World Bank published its notorious report, *Accelerated Development for Africa: an Agenda for Africa*. It certainly was an agenda for Africa, set by the erstwhile Bretton Woods institutions (BWIs) with the backing of Western countries. But it had little to do with development, accelerated or otherwise. The report and subsequent structural adjustment programmes concentrated on stabilisation measures: eliminating budget deficits, bringing down inflation rates, getting prices right, unleashing the free market and liberalising trade.

According to the World Bank, the villain of the declining economic performance in Africa was the state: it was corrupt and dictatorial with no capacity to manage the economy and allocate resources rationally. It was bloated with bureaucracy; its mode of operation was nepotism. The BWIs refused to bail out the crisis-ridden economies unless the governments adopted structural adjustment programmes that ensured stabilisation fundamentals.

Balancing budgets involved cutting agricultural subsidies and spending on social programmes including education and health. Unleashing the free market meant doing away with the protection of infant industries and rolling back the state in economic activity. The results of structural adjustment have been devastating, as many studies have shown. Social indicators show that education, medical care, health, nutrition, rates of literacy and life expectancy have all declined. De-industrialisation and redundancies have ensued. Even some of the most modest achievements of the nationalist or developmentalist period were lost or undermined (Gibbon 1993, 1995) (Adedeji 1993).

As the international situation changed with the collapse of the Soviet Union, Western imperialist powers regained the ideological initiative. The neoliberal package of marketisation, privatisation and liberalisation became the policy for (but not of) African states. Good performers were praised and rewarded with more aid while the insubordinate and recalcitrant were parodied, left to their own resources. Whilst aid had always come with strings, there was no longer any attempt to disguise it.

Political conditionalities – multi-party democracy, good governance, human rights etc – were added to economic conditionalities. Decision-making and policy making slipped out of the hands of African states as the West financed policy and governance consultants in their thousands to produce policy blue prints, poverty reduction strategies and manuals on good governance. This absorbed some US\$4 billion annually. In 1985, to give just one example, foreign experts resident in Equatorial Guinea were paid three times the total government public sector wage bill (Mkandawire & Soludo 1999).

National liberation ideologies have been rubbished and

21

national self-determination declared passé. Africa is told it has only one choice: integrate fully into the globalised world, or remain marginalised. The spectre of marginalisation is so rampant that even progressive African scholars are daring to say that 'Africa may be graduating from being the region with "lost development decades" to becoming the world's forgotten continent' (Mkandawire & Soludo).

The former US ambassador to Tanzania, my country, speaking to lawmakers was blatant about what the superpower expected of African states:

> The liberation diplomacy of the past, when alliances with socialist nations were paramount and so-called Third World Solidarity dominated foreign policy, must give way to a more realistic approach to dealing with your true friends – those who are working to lift you into the twenty-first century, where poverty is not acceptable and disease must be conquered.[2]

African leaders are left with little option: 'you are either with globalisation or doomed!' They have fallen into line, one after another, even if it has meant disowning their own past. The report of Tony Blair's Commission for Africa, which consisted of prominent Africans, including one president and one prime minister, castigates the last three decades in their entirety – which virtually means the whole of the post-independence period – as 'lost decades' (Graham 2005). The primary responsibility for bad governance and lack of accountability is placed on the African state. The report totally ignores the role of imperialism in both the exploitation of African resources and in lending support to non-democratic states when it suited their interests. Africans are told they have no capacity to think. African states are told they have no capacity to formulate correct policies. As the commission (p. 14) declared – with a straight face (emphasis in the original):

> Africa's history over the last fifty years has been blighted by two areas of weakness. These have been *capacity* – the ability to design and deliver policies; and *accountability* – how well a state answers to its people.

So, policy-making, an important aspect of sovereignty, has been wrenched out of the hands of the African state, which is placed on the same level as other so-called stakeholders, including NGOs.

The fundamental premises of globalisation or neoliberalism

Globalisation in Africa is manifest in the neoliberal economic and political packages, centering around trade liberalisation, privatisation of national assets and resources, commodification of social services and marketisation of goods and services, both tangible and intangible.

In sum, the underlying thrust of neoliberal and globalised development 'discourse' is for a deeper integration of African economies into global capital and market circuits, without fundamental transformation. It is predicated on private capital, which in Africa translates into foreign

private capital, as the 'engine of growth'. It centres on economic growth, without questioning whether growth necessarily translates into development.

It banishes issues of equality and equity to the realm of rights, not development. And 'rights' are reduced to the purview of advocacy NGOs, no longer a terrain for popular struggle. 'Human-centered' or 'people-driven' development approaches, previously the kingpins of African alternatives, such as the Lagos Plan of Action, are pooh-poohed into non-existence. Development falls within the purview of development practitioners and development NGOs, which advocate right-based development.

The African people, who were once supposed to be the authors and drivers of development and liberators of their nations, are reduced to the category of 'the chronically poor'. They become the subject matter of poverty reduction strategy papers, authored by consultants, and discussed at stakeholder workshops in which the 'poor' are represented by NGOs. The 'poor' – the diseased, the disabled, the Aids-infected, the ignorant, the marginalised, in short the 'people' – are not part of the development equation, since development is assigned to the private capital that constitutes the 'engine of growth'. The 'poor' are the recipients of humanitarian aid provided by 'true friends', (thanks to the American ambassador for that phraseology), dispensed by non-partisan, non-political, presumably non-involved, non-governmental organisations. In these societies, where stakeholders never tire of policy-making for the poor, its twin opposite – the rich – do not appear to exist. It is said that these societies consist only of the poor and the wealth creators, not of producers and appropriators of wealth.

In this neoliberal discourse, the African state is cast as villain. African bureaucracies are demonised as corrupt, incapable and unable to learn. Thus they need globalised foreign advisors and consultants, now termed development practitioners, to mentor, monitor and oversee them. Among the mentors and monitors are of course the NGOs. The so-called advisors and consultants move freely between the triad family consisting of the 'DONs' (donor organisations), the 'INFOs' (international financial organisations) and the NGOs, including 'GoNGOs' (government-organised NGOs) and the 'DoNGOs' (donor-organised NGOs).

In this 'discourse' the developmental role of the state is declared dead and buried. Instead, it is assigned the role of 'chief' to supervise the globalisation project under the tutelage of imperial – now called development – partners or 'true friends'. The irony of the recent British Commission for Africa was that it was convened, constituted and chaired by a British prime minister, while an African president and a prime minister sat on it as members. This symbolises the nature of the so-called 'new partnership'. The message is clear: African 'co-partners' in African development are neither equal nor in the driving seat.[3]

It is true that the neoliberal discourse has not gone without challenge, both intellectual and practical. African people have fought on the streets against structural adjustment policies. They have protested in their villages, towns and neighborhoods. African intellectuals have written and argued to illustrate the fallacy of the underlying assumptions of neoliberalism and globalisation.

Yet, it is also true, at least for the time being, that

25

neoliberalism is holding sway. Virtually the whole of the African political elite and establishment have fallen into line (unlike, for example, in Latin America) whether for pragmatic reasons of survival, or else to defend their own vested interests. A large part of the African intellectual elite has been co-opted and accommodated within the neoliberal discourse.

This paper argues that the sudden rise of NGOs and their apparently prominent role in Africa are part of this neoliberal, organisational and ideological offensive.

NGOs or the so-called 'third sector'

At the inception of the neoliberal offensive in the early 1980s, the rise and role of NGOs were explained and justified within the conceptual framework of the problematic of civil society. The concept of civil society came into vogue in the 1980s, during the collapse of the Soviet and East European systems, and the democratisation drive in Africa. In Eastern Europe, following the collapse of bureaucratic socialist regimes (or actually existing socialism, as they were then christened), the construction of civil societies was seen as returning to 'normal society on the Western model'. In Eastern Europe itself, the term has been used in as many different ways as contexts (Shivji 2002).

Civil society discourse in Africa has also used the term with all kinds of meanings: from associational connotations ('civil societies') to all-virtuous, harmonious social spaces. But it is in the meaning of free associations, 'independent' of the state, that the term has stuck. Very often the term 'civil society organisation' (CSO) is used interchangeably with NGO.

Influenced heavily, as always, by US based Africanists, a false bipolarity or dichotomy between state and civil society has predominated. Within the neoliberal ideologies, the state is demonised. Civil society, often conflated with the NGOs, is privileged. NGOs are presented as the 'third sector', the other two sectors being the state – power, politics, and the private sector – capital, economics. This ideological presentation of NGO also dominates self-perception in the NGO world itself. Yet it is based on utterly false historical and intellectual premises and posits serious political implications (Shivji 2002).

The concept of civil society in European history represented the transition from a medieval feudalist to a capitalist society. This was part of the bourgeois revolution. In that context, civil society was, for both Hegel and Marx and perhaps even for Weber, an ensemble of free, equal and abstract individuals associating in the public sphere of production as opposed to the private sphere of the family. For Marx, civil society was synonymous with bourgeois society. The concept is developed in opposition to feudal relations where the public and the private are merged, and statuses are determined by birth and privileges and where politics is direct, 'that is to say, the elements of civil life, for example, property, or the family, or the mode of labour were raised to the level of political life in the form of seignority, estates, and corporations' (Sayers 1991, p. 75).

At the same time for Marx – and this is directly relevant to our conceptual debate about civil society – whereas civil society presents itself as an ensemble of free individuals and as a separate sphere from the state or politics, it is in

27

fact the soil from which state power arises, and in which it is embedded. For our purpose, it is necessary to highlight two conclusions. First, the so-called civil society, in the sense of the public sphere of production, is not a harmonious whole; rather a terrain of contradictory relations

> The colonial infrastructure was the exact antithesis of a national economy. The only rationale behind individual African countries as loci of national independence was the fact that each one of them fell under the jurisdiction of a different colonial power... The ideological genesis of African nationalism lay in pan-Africanism. The locus of pan-Africanism was the continent itself, not the artificially created spaces bound by colonial borders called countries.

between classes – the two poles being the producer class and the appropriator class. Second, the separation between state and civil society, between economics and politics, is ideological. It is how the bourgeois society appears and presents itself. In reality, those who command and control the sphere of production also wield political power – that is the state.

28

When applied to colonial society, we find that the colonial sphere of production is essentially controlled by imperial capital. The colonial mode of production is characterised by the extraction of surplus from non-capitalist classes through the use of state force. The national bourgeois project promised by the independence movement is aborted and defeated. In the 1960s and 1970s, there was a great debate among Third World intellectuals as to whether a national bourgeois project could ever succeed in the Third World, particularly in Africa, in an era of imperialism (Amin 1990) (Tandon 1982) (Mahjoub 1990).

Be that as it may, the transformation from a colonial subject society to a bourgeois civil society in Africa is incomplete, stunted and distorted. We have the continued domination of imperialism – reproduction of the colonial mode – in a different form, currently labelled globalisation or neoliberalism. Within this context, NGOs are neither a third sector, nor independent of the state. Rather they are inextricably imbricated in the neoliberal offensive, which follows on the heels of the crisis of the national project. Unless there is awareness on the part of the NGOs of this fundamental moment in the struggle between imperialism and nationalism, they end up playing the role of ideological and organisational foot soldiers of imperialism, however this is described.

Below, I demonstrate how five silences in the NGO discourse contribute to the mystification and obfuscation of the role of NGOs.

The five silences

What are NGOs?

To preface this section, I provide a quick factual summary of the salient features of NGOs in the African setting.

Firstly, a large number of African NGOs were born in the womb of the neoliberal offensive which began to open up space for freedom of association. One feature of the statist period was the organisational hegemony of the state. In the first flush of the opening up of organisational space, NGOs proliferated without critical examination of the place and role of NGOs, and their underlying ideologies and premises. The anti-state stance of the so-called donor-community was the real push behind the upsurge in NGO activity.

Secondly, NGOs are led by and largely composed of the educated elite. They are located in urban areas and well-versed in the language and idiom of modernisation. Broadly three types of NGO-elites may be identified.

The first category is the radical elite that was previously involved in political struggles, with an explicit vision for change and transformation, but which found itself suppressed under the statist hegemony. Many of these elites took the opportunity to express themselves politically in the NGOs. They saw NGOs as a possible terrain of struggle for change. This section of the elite is essentially politically motivated, without being necessarily involved in partisan, party-politics.

The second category includes well-intentioned individuals driven by altruistic motives to improve the conditions of their fellow human beings and compatriots. In other words, they are morally motivated.

The third category is the mainstream elite, not infrequently former government bureaucrats, who shifted to the NGO world once they found that donor funding was being directed there. The motivation of this elite is simply careerist. It is driven by material gains, rather than altruism. It is personally motivated. This category keeps swelling as jobs in the state and private sector become more and more competitive or difficult to come by.

Thirdly, an overwhelming number of NGOs are donor funded. They do not have any independent source of funding. They have to seek donor funds through customary procedures set by the funding agencies. In this respect, the degree of independence they can exercise in relation to donor agendas varies from NGO to NGO depending on the perspectives of its leadership. In practice though, as would be readily acknowledged by even the most radical among them, their scope for action is limited.

This does not necessarily mean that a few may not exercise greater autonomy in their outlook and ideology and still be accepted; exceptions are necessary to prove the rule.

While some NGOs may be quite involved with and appreciated by the people whom they purport to serve, ultimately NGOs, by their very nature, derive not only their sustenance but also their legitimacy from the donor-community. In the current international conjuncture, even political elites located in the state or political parties seek legitimacy from so-called 'development-partners', rather than from their own people. Not surprisingly, there is a fair amount of circulation of the elite between government and

31

 SILENCES IN NGO DISCOURSE

non-governmental sectors.

Fourthly, by far the greatest number of NGOs are advocacy NGOs focusing on particular areas of activity such as human rights, gender, development, environment and governance. There are always NGOs set up by politically or morally motivated individuals with genuine desire to 'do something', and which are genuinely meant to respond to the need of the people. But it is also true that a substantial number of NGOs are set up to respond to whatever is perceived to be in vogue among the donor-community at any particular time. Donor-driven NGOs, I would guess, are perhaps the most dominant.

Besides advocacy tasks, NGOs are also increasingly commissioned by donors, or the state or even the corporate sector, to undertake consultancy work, or be their executive agencies to dispense funds or services. Thus NGOs have come to play a major role in the aid industry. In the NGO world, it is not at all ironical that a non-governmental body is assigned by the government to do a governmental job and is funded by a donor agency, which in turn is an outfit of a foreign government. Thus USAID may fund a gender NGO to raise awareness among women about a new land law whose terms of reference are set by a government ministry. To complete the picture, one may find that the same USAID may have recommended and sponsored a consultant who drafted the land law for the government in the first place.

Fifth, while most NGOs may insert in their charters a vision or mission statement, these are often vague, amorphous and meaningless – for example 'poverty-reduction'. In any case, they are quickly forgotten. What takes over are the so-called strategic plans and log-frames which can be tabulated, quantified and ticked for triennium reports and proposals for more funding. The 'success' of an NGO is measured by how efficiently it is managed and run. The criteria for measuring efficiency are borrowed from the corporate sector. Training NGOs are set up to train NGO managers in 'strategic framework analysis', in charting 'inputs' and 'outcomes' tables, in setting indicators and in methods and techniques to log the vision and the mission and the strategy in log-frames. As Brian Murphy observes (Murphy 2001, pp. 74 & 80):

> This ethos has been embraced by and is now aggressively – sometimes ruthlessly – promoted by senior managers in many of our leading NGOs, convinced that restructuring our organisations along corporate lines is the ticket to successful integration in the new trilateral global order that sees the public, private, and voluntary sectors somehow as partners in development. ... Increasingly the model for the 'successful' NGO is the corporation – ideally a transnational corporation and NGOs are ever more marketed and judged against corporate ideals. As part of the trend, a new development scientism is strangling us with things like strategic framework analysis and results-based management, precisely the values and methods and techniques that have made the world what it is today.

Below, I illustrate how the rise, role and features of NGOs, which objectively situate them within the imperial project,

are reinforced by certain 'silences' in NGO discourse.

Privileging activism or changing the world without understanding it

During the revolutionary moment of the 1960s and 1970s, when the national liberation movement was at its height, it used to be said that we should 'think globally and act locally'. This summed up four fundamental ideas. One, imperialism was global and oppressed all peoples world-wide. So it must be understood in its global context. Two, imperialism would have to be fought at the level of its local manifestations. The concrete analysis of the concrete situation was underlined. Three, the slogan expressed the international solidarity of all peoples across the globe against imperialism. Four, imperialism had to be clearly understood and correctly described in all aspects so as to conduct an organised and conscious struggle against it.

These assumptions informed the basis of profound intellectual debates on the theory and practice of imperialism and national liberation. As Amilcar Cabral, one of the foremost leaders of the African liberation movement, put it: 'every practice produces a theory...if it is true that a revolution can fail even though it be based on perfectly conceived theories, nobody has yet made a successful revolution without a revolutionary theory' (Cabral 1969, p. 75).

What is interesting about that period is that radical intellectual discourse was integrated with militant activism; the two were mutually reinforcing. The NGO discourse in the current period of apparent imperial 'triumphalism' eschews theory, and emphasises and privileges activism. In the African setting in particular, whatever is left of critical intellectual discourse, largely located in the universities, runs parallel to and is divorced from NGO activism. The requirements of funding agencies subtly discourage, if not exhibiting outright hostility to a historical, social and theoretical understanding of development, poverty and discrimination. Our erstwhile benefactors now tell us: 'just act, don't think'; and we shall fund both.

The report of Tony Blair's Commission for Africa castigates the last three decades in their entirety as 'lost decades'. The primary responsibility for bad governance and lack of accountability is placed on the African state. The report totally ignores the role of imperialism in both the exploitation of African resources and in lending support to non-democratic states when it suited their interests.

The inherent bias against theory is manifested at various levels. I will mention a couple. First, the penchant for project funding, which is supposed to be operated and completed within a given time – a triennium for example – does not admit thinking about the underlying premises of the so-called project. The managerial techniques of monitoring and evaluating projects through log-frames by

their very nature compartmentalise and dissect life to such an extent that the sight of the whole, even the capacity to think holistically, is lost.

Secondly, the projects are issue-based and are supposed to be addressed as issues. The issue itself is identified as a problem at the level of phenomenon; its underlying basis is not addressed but assumed. The issue is isolated and abstracted from its social, economic and historical reality; therefore, its interconnectedness to other issues and the whole is lost.

Thirdly, issue-oriented and time-limited projects do not allow for any long-term basic research based on solid theoretical and historical premises. So-called research by NGOs or consultants (rather than researchers), if it relates to anything at all, relates to policy and not to the social, economic and political interests underlying the phenomenon under investigation. Nor does it relate to how these interests reproduce themselves. Thus 'research' by consultants degenerates into rapid appraisals, not much more than opinion polls.

In sum, NGO activism is presented and based on the 'act now, think later' mantra. Theory, and particularly grand theory, is dismissed as academicism, unworthy of activists. Yet, we know, that every practice gives rise to theory and that every action is based on some theoretical or philosophical premise or outlook. NGO action is also based on certain theoretical premises and philosophical outlooks. In their case however, theory is written off as 'common sense' and therefore not interrogated.

I believe I have shown sufficiently that the 'common sense' theoretical assumption of the current period underpinning NGO roles and actions is neoliberalism in the interest of global imperialism. It is fundamentally contrary to the interests of the large majority of the people. Taking for granted the fundamentals of neoliberalism and financial capitalism, or challenging them only piecemeal on specific issues, for example debt, environment or gender discrimination, actually draws the NGOs as protagonists into the imperial project. Brian Murphy argues that many mainstream NGO leaders have internalised assumptions and ways of neo-conservatism, and are convinced that globalisation akin to neoliberalism are inevitable and irreversible. Thus they have joined 'its acolytes, ironically without much critical analysis of what "it" actually is or means'. He continues: 'What the corporate PR manager understands implicitly as economic propaganda, NGO people often repeat as articles of faith' (Murphy 2001, p. 81).

The permanent present

Of late, African poverty has been brought to the centre stage of the NGO world, ironically by the likes of imperial leaders such as Tony Blair. The African NGO world echoes and repeats the slogan generated by their Northern benefactors: 'Make Poverty History'. But how can you make poverty history without understanding the history of poverty? We need to know how the poverty of the five billion of this world came about. Even more acutely, we need to know how the filthy wealth of the 500 multinationals or the 225 richest people was created (Peacock 2002). We need to know precisely how this great divide, this unbridgeable chasm, is maintained; how it reproduced itself, and how it is increasingly deepened and widened. We need to ask

37

 SILENCES IN NGO DISCOURSE

ourselves: What are the political, social, moral, ideological, economic and cultural mechanisms which produce, reinforce and make such a world not only possible, but seemingly acceptable?

Yet, the NGO discourse seems to have internalised the thoughtless idiocies of right-wing reactionary writers such as Francis Fukuyama who propagate the 'end of history' in which the present – that is, of course, the present global capitalism under the hegemony of the imperialist North – is declared permanent. Any historical understanding of our present state is ridiculed and dismissed, or tolerated as a token in order to create the illusion of 'diversity'. In the African setting, any discussion of colonial history invariably elicits the standard responses: stop blaming the colonialists. How long shall we continue lamenting colonialism? Thus history is reduced to a blaming exercise and ridiculed.

However, as I have sketched out, colonial and imperial history are at the heart of the present African condition. History is not about assigning or sharing blame. Nor it is about narrating the 'past', which must be forgotten and forgiven, or simply remembered once a year on remembrance of heroes or independence days. History is about the present. We must understand the present as history, so as to change it for the better; perforce, in the African context where the imperial project is not only historical, but the lived present. Just as we cannot 'make poverty history' without understanding the history of poverty, so we cannot chant 'another world is possible' without accurately understanding and correctly describing the existing world of five billion slaves and 200 slave masters. How did it come about and how does it continue to exist? Indeed to answer these questions, we must understand history as the philosophy and political economy that underpin the existing world and the vested interests – real social interests of real people – that ensure and defend its existence.

Society as a harmonious whole of stakeholders

Much of the NGO discourse is based on the following premises, inherent in the liberal capitalist world outlook and its new globalisation variant. First, the separation of self and society, where society is seen as an aggregate sum of atomic individuals. Second, the liberal goal is to privilege individual interests which are knowable and ascertainable (individual self-determination in the language of post-modernism), assuming that social interests would thus have been taken care of. In the post-modernist variant, social interests are in any case unknowable. Third, that the social whole is presented as a harmonious whole in which there is a range of more or less equal but diverse interests. The premise that social interests are not all at the same level, that some are dominant and in conflict with others, is eschewed.

The neoliberal model of development based on private property and accumulation, the market as the motor of society, commodification of resources, services and basic needs is taken as 'common sense', requiring no further proof. In Africa, this translates into further and deeper integration of economies into the global capital and market circuits; the opening up of natural wealth and resources for the exploitation of voracious transnational corporations; and outlawing resistance as, at best, aberrant or outdated,

 SILENCES IN NGO DISCOURSE

at worst 'terrorist'.

Thus is derived the basis of the so-called triad of stake-holders – the state, the private sector and the voluntary sector. The state is presented as the neutral referee, the guarantor of law and order, whose main function is to provide stability and an enabling environment for private capital. Private capital is the main engine or motor of growth, which will eventually trickle down to the whole of society. In this drive for inexorable growth and progress, it is acknowledged that some will inevitably be left behind, marginalised, or simply unable to cope: the so-called poor.

Therefore the voluntary sector is needed to take care of them. Social welfare and provision of basic needs and services to the community are no longer the responsibility of the state or the private sector; instead they are assigned to NGOs. Thus the 'holy trinity' of development partners is completed: state, capital and NGOs, the latter suppos-edly the major stakeholders in participatory development enterprise.

The net effect is the legitimisation of the essentially exploitative capitalist system presented as pro-poor and morally driven by the so-called NGO sector. The progressive agenda of people-driven development – the radical, popu-list agenda of the nationalists of yesteryear – is co-opted. In effect, therefore, we see a re-enactment of the missionary positions of the colonial time where church, charity and cat-echists played the legitimising role in the colonial enterprise, duping the colonised and damning the freedom fighters. The role assigned to NGOs is in principle not very different, whatever the secular, universal and globalised platitudes are in which it is articulated: 'global neighbourhood', 'global village', 'global citizenship' (Manji & O'Coill 2002). Just as the colonial enterprise assumed the garb of a civilising mission and used the church as its avant-garde, so the globalisation pundits speak the language of secular human rights, using the NGOs as their ideological foot soldiers.

The international and national orders within which we are functioning are unequal and there are conflicting interests. To pretend that society is a harmonious whole of stakeholders is to be complicit in perpetuating the status quo in the interest of the dominant classes and powers. In the struggle between national liberation and imperialist domination, and between social emancipation and capitalist slavery, NGOs have to choose sides. In this there are no in-betweens.

Non-governmental equals non-political?

The separation between politics and economics, between state and civil society is how the bourgeois society appears and presents itself. But it is not its real essence. In reality, politics is the quintessence, or the concentrated form of economics. The political sphere is built on the sphere of production, and there is a close relationship between those who command production and those who wield power. Yet the NGO sector, which according to its own proclamations stands for change, accepts the ideological myth that it is the third sector: non-political, not-for-profit, having nothing to do with power or production. This bourgeois mythology mystifies the reality of capitalist production and power, thus contributing to its legitimisation. NGOs by accepting the myth of being non-political contribute to the process of mystification, and therefore objectively side with the status

quo, contrary to their expressed stand for change.

Ironically, the non-political NGOs are involved in the process of so-called policy-making. They participate in, or are made to feel that they participate in, policy-making and policy dialogue among stakeholders. This has several implications. First, policy-making, an attribute of sovereignty for which the government of the day is supposedly accountable to its people, is wrenched from the state and vested in the amorphous coterie of 'development partners'

...colonial and imperial history are at the heart of the present African condition... we must understand the present as history, so as to change it for the better; perforce, in the African context where the imperial project is not only historical, but the lived present

---

or stakeholders. Everyone knows who the determining stakeholder really is. The old adage applies: he who pays the piper calls the tune.

Second, the notion that NGOs really participate in policy-making is an illusion. In this day and age of donor-driven policies, this applies equally to the African state itself. Thirdly, it is presumptuous on the part of NGOs to pretend that they represent the people in the process of policy-making. Fourthly, the whole process undermines the supposedly democratic and representative character of the state. As the state abdicates responsibility for 'its' policies, ceasing to be accountable to its own people, it becomes accountable instead to the so-called development partners.

Finally, the process of policy-making, a political process par excellence, is presented as if it were a neutral non-political exercise in which non-political NGOs may participate without losing non-partisanship. Needless to say, policy-making is a terrain of intense conflicts of interest, and has nothing neutral about it. The question is, as always, which interest is being served by a particular policy. A question about which there can be neither neutrality nor non-partisanship.

What is a better or alternative world?

'A better world is possible' according to the NGO slogan. But to build a better world we must understand the world better. This then is my message. 'An alternative world is possible' is another adage of the NGOs. But the underlying question remains: what would such an alternative world in the current African context look like? I have tried to argue that Africa is at the crossroads of the defeat of the national project and the reassertion of the imperial project. The national liberation struggles of the 1960s and 1970s, which put imperialism on the ideological defensive, have been aborted. Imperialism by the name of globalisation is returning, while refurbishing its moral and ideological image. Or at least it is in the process of refurbishing its image. NGOs were born in the womb of neoliberalism and knowingly or otherwise are participating in the imperial project.

There is little doubt that there are very fine and dedicated people in the NGOs, genuinely committed to the struggle for a better world. But there are serious blind spots and silences in NGO discourse, which objectively result in the NGO world participating in the imperial, rather than in the national project. NGOs cannot be pro-people and pro-change without being anti-imperialist and anti-status quo.

Arguably, NGOs must engage in critical discourse and political activism rather than assume false neutrality and non-partisanship. In this perspective, African NGOs need to build bridges with African intellectuals and scholars where there is a serious debate, albeit on the fringes of the mainstream, about the 'alternative African world'. Currently, under another false dichotomy between activism and intellectualism, critical intellectual discourse runs parallel to NGO discourse. We need therefore to bring together African activism and African intellectualism in a dialogue that critically interrogates both 'our' comprado-rial states and their imperial masters.

Conclusion

To conclude, I will briefly sketch some of the thinking that is emerging among critical scholarship in Africa and where we stand in the struggle towards pan-African liberation, social justice and human emancipation.

We must first record that the neoliberal project in Africa has not been accepted without practical and intellectual resistance. In a preface to a book by African scholars significantly subtitled *Beyond Dispossession and Dependence*,

Nyerere observed: 'Africa's history is not only one of slavery, exploitation and colonialism; it is also a story of struggle against these evils, and of battles won after many setbacks and much suffering' (Adedeji 1993, p. xv).

Just as the African people have struggled and opposed structural adjustment in the streets, African intellectuals have critically scrutinised its neoliberal underpinnings and exposed globalisation as a new form of imperialism. African NGOs must creatively appropriate these intellectual insights. They must learn from the actually existing struggles of the people before evangelising on donor-fads of the day: gender, human rights, female genital mutilation, good governance, etc. The educators must first be educated.

Secondly, critically interrogating the national project, African scholars have noted the resurgence of nationalism and observed both its positive and negative aspects. The first lesson is that the African national project located at the territorial level is bound to fail. African nationalism, as some of the fathers of African nationalism realised, is and must be pan-African. Pan-Africanism, they argue, is the nationalism of the era of globalisation; and only pan-Africanism can carry forward the struggle for national liberation in Africa. Without a pan-African vision, there is the danger that the resurgence of nationalism as a reaction to the new imperial assault could degenerate into narrow, parochial, nationalist chauvinism, even ethnicism and racism (Shivji 2005) (Yieke 2005).

But this new pan-Africanism must be a bottom-up people's pan-Africanism, and not a top-down statist pan-Africanism. In the hands of the African state and its 'lead-

45

ers', pan-Africanism will degenerate into 'NEPAD-ism', or phony African renaissance (Landsberg & Kornegey 1998). The New Partnership for African Development (NEPAD), as the name itself suggests, is a donor-dependent programme seeking more aid and assistance from the erstwhile 'international community', predicated on further integration of Africa into unequal global structures (Nyong'o et al 2002). A 'feudo-imperial partnership', the objective of NEPAD is 'for the African canoe to be firmly tied to the North's neoliberal ship on the waters of globalisation', according to Adebayo Adedeji (Nyong'o 2002).

Thirdly, a fundamental transformation of African societies – an African revolution if you like – is very much on the agenda. The nature of this revolution is very much debated. It is suggested though that it must be a revolution that is thoroughly anti-imperialist and consistently pro-people: a revolution based on popular power, fighting for and defending popular livelihoods, predicated on popular participation (Mafeje 2002) (Shivji 2000).

Fourthly, actually existing states in Africa are essentially compradorised; that is, they are neither democratic nor pro-people. States themselves must be restructured and reorganised with roots in the people and seeking legitimacy from the people rather than from a consortia of G8 ('the global gobblers') imperial powers otherwise known as the 'international community'.

Fifthly, the African people must recover their sovereignty and self-determination: their right to think for themselves and in genuine solidarity with the oppressed people of the world.

Above all, I would submit that there is a need to integrate intellectual and activist discourse. Only then can NGOs truly play the role of catalysts of change rather than catechists of aid and charity. Indeed, the potential of the NGO sector to play such a role has been demonstrated, albeit in infancy, in such struggles as the Seattle street fights against the world's foremost imperial institutions, and the demonstrations condemning the invasion of Iraq against the world's foremost and most brutal superpower.

If NGOs are to play that role, they must fundamentally re-examine their silences and their discourses. They must scrutinise the philosophical and political premises that underpin their activities. They must investigate the credentials of their development partners and the motives of their financial benefactors. They must distance themselves from oppressive African states and compradorial ruling elites. NGOs must refuse to legitimise, rationalise and provide a veneer of respectability and morality for global pillage carried out by voracious transnationals under the tag line of 'creating a global village'.

Because I dare say that if we in the NGO world did understand the history of poverty and enslavement in Africa, if we did scrutinise the credentials of so-called development partners, if we did distance ourselves from the oppressive African state, if we did refuse to lend our names to poverty reduction polices and strategies, meant to legitimise the filthy rich, if, indeed, we vowed to be catalysts of change and refused to be catechist of charity, we would have been toyi-toyi-ing at the doorsteps of Blair and his commissioners, beating our tom-toms and singing 'make imperialism history' instead of jumping on the bandwagon of Sir Bob Geldof's Band Aid.

SILENCES IN NGO DISCOURSE

References

Adedeji, A., ed. 1993, *Africa within the World: Beyond Dispossession and Dependence*, London: Zed

Amin, S., 1990, *Maldevelopment: Anatomy of a Global Failure*, London: Zed

Blum, W., 1986, *The CIA, a Forgotten History*, London: Zed

Blum, W., 2001, *Rogue State, A Guide to the World's Only Superpower*, London: Zed

Bond, P., ed. 2002, *Fanon's Warning: a Civil Society Reader on the New Partnership for Africa's Development*, New Jersey: Africa World Press

Cabral, A., 1969, 'The weapon of theory', in Amilcar Cabral, *Revolution in Guinea*, London: Stage 1

Cabral, A., 1980, *Unity and Struggle: Speeches and Writings*, London: Heinemann

Campbell, H., & H. Stein, eds., 1991, *The IMF and Tanzania*, Harare: SAPES

Davidson, B., 1961, *Black Mother: A Study of the Precolonial Connection between Africa and Europe*, London: Longman

De Witte, L., 2001, *The Assassination of Lumumba*, Johannesburg: Jacana

Fanon, F., 1963, *The Wretched of the Earth*, London: Penguin

Furedi, F., 1994, *The New Ideology of Imperialism*, London: Pluto Press

Graham, Y., 2005, 'Africa's second 'last chance', Red Pepper/G8 Africa Commission, http://www.redpepper.org.uk/global/x-jul05-graham.htm

Himmelstrand, U. et al. eds., 1994, *African Perspectives on Development*, Oxford: James Currey

Kjekshus, H., 1977 & 1996, *Ecology Control and Economic Development in East African History*, Oxford: James Currey

Landsberg, C. & F. Kornegey, 1998, 'The African Renaissance: a quest for Pax Africana and Pan-Africanism', *South Africa and Africa:*

Reflections on the African Renaissance, Foundation for Global Dialogue, Occasional paper No. 17

Legum, L., 1965, *Pan-Africanism: A Short Political Guide*, (Revised edition) London: Pall Mall Press

Mafeje, A., 2002, 'Democratic governance and new democracy in Africa: Agenda for the Future', in Nyong'o, Ghirmazion & Lamba, eds. 2002, *New Partnership for Africa's Development, NEPAD: A New Path?* Nairobi: Heinrich Boll Foundation

Mahjoub, A., 1990, *Adjustment or De-linking?* London: Zed/UNU

Mamdani, M., 1987, 'Contradictory class perspectives on the question of democracy', in Peter Anyang' Nyongo, ed., *Popular Struggles for Democracy in Africa*, London: United Nations University/Zed

Mamdani, M., 1996, *Citizen and Subject: Contemporary Africa and the Legacy of Late Colonialism*, Princeton: Princeton University Press

Manji, F. & Carol O'Coill, 2002, 'The missionary position: NGOs and development in Africa' in *International Affairs* 78,3:567-83

Mboya, T., *Freedom and After*, 1963, London: Andre Deutsch

Mkandawire, T. & C. C. Soludo, eds., 1999, *Our Continent, Our Future: African Perspectives on Structural Adjustment*, Dakar: CODESRIA

Murphy, B. K., 2001, 'International NGOs and the challenge of modernity', in Deborah Eade & Ernst Ligteringen eds., *Debating Development*, Oxford: Oxfam GB

Mwaikusa, J. T., 1995, *Towards Responsible Democratic Government: Executive Power and Constitutional Practice in Tanzania, 1962-1992*, Ph.D. dissertation, University of London

Nkrumah, K., 1965, *Neo-colonialism: The Last Stage of Imperialism*, London: Heinemann

Nyerere, J. K., 1963a, 'A United States of Africa', *Journal of Modern African Studies*, January 1963, Cambridge reprinted in Nyerere op. cit. 1967

Nyerere, J. K., 1963b, 'The Second Scramble', reprinted in Nyerere

 SILENCES IN NGO DISCOURSE

op. cit. 1967

Nyerere, J.K., 1966, 'The Dilemma of the Pan-Africanist,' in J. K. Nyerere, op. cit. 1968

Nyerere, J. K., 1967, *Freedom and Unity: A Selection from Writings and Speeches*, Dar es Salaam: Oxford University Press

Nyerere, J. K., 1968, *Freedom and Socialism*, London: Oxford University Press

Nyerere, J.K., 1997, 'Africa Must Unite', edited excerpts from a public lecture delivered in Accra to mark Ghana's fortieth Independence Day anniversary celebrations, United New Africa Global Network,<http://www.unitednewafrica.com/Africa%20Unite.htm>

Nyong'o, Ghirmazion & Lamba, eds. 2002, *New Partnership for Africa's Development*, NEPAD: A New Path? Nairobi: Heinrich Boll Foundation

Peacock, A., 2002, *Two Hundred Pharaohs and Five Billion Slaves*, London

Rodney, W., 1972, *How Europe Underdeveloped Africa*, Dar es Salaam: Tanzania Publishing House

Sayers, D., 1991, *Capitalism & Modernity: An Excursus on Marx and Weber*, London: Routledge

Semboja, J., Juma, Mwapachu & Eduard Jansen eds., 2002. *Local Perspectives on Globalisation: The African Case*, Dar es Salaam: REPOA & Mkuki na Nyota Publishers

Sheriff, A., 1987, *Slaves, Spices & Ivory in Zanzibar*, London: James Currey

Shivji, I. G., 1987, 'The roots of the agrarian crisis in Tanzania', *Eastern Africa Social Science Research Review*, vol. 111, no.1:111-134

Shivji, I. G., ed., 1991, *State and Constitutionalism: An African Debate on Democracy*, Harare: SAPES

Shivji, I. G., 1998, *Not Yet Democracy: Reforming Land Tenure in Tanzania*, London: IIED

Shivji, I. G., 2000, 'Critical Elements of a New Democratic Consensus in Africa' in Haroub Othman (ed.) *Reflections on Leadership in Africa: Essays in Honour of Mwalimu Julius K. Nyerere*, Belgium: VUB University Press

Shivji, I.G., 2002, 'Globalisation and Popular Resistance' in Joseph Semboja, Juma Mwapachu & Eduard Jansen, eds. *Local Perspectives on Globalisation: The African Case*, Dar es Salaam: REPOA, Mkuki na Nyota

Shivji, I. G., 2003, 'Three generations of constitutions and constitution-making in Africa: An overview and assessment in social and economic context', in M. S. Rosen ed., *Constitutionalism in Transition: Africa and Eastern Europe*, Helsinki Foundation for Human Rights

Shivji, I. G., 2005a, 'The Rise, the Fall and the Insurrection of Nationalism in Africa', in Felicia Arudo Yieke ed. op.cit.

Shivji, I.G., 2005b, 'Pan-Africanism or Imperialism?' 2nd Billy Dudley Memorial Lecture to the Nigerian Political Science Association, Nsukka, Nigeria, July 2005

Tandon, Y., 1982, *University of Dar es Salaam: Debate on Class, State & Imperialism*, Dar es Salaam: Tanzania Publishing House

Wamba, E., 1991, 'Discourse on the National Question', in I. G. Shivji, ed. *State and Constitutionalism: An African Debate on Democracy*, Harare: SAPES

Wamba, E., 1996, 'The National Question in Zaire: Challenges to the Nation-State Project', in Adebayo O. Olukoshi & Liisa Laakso, eds. *Challenges to the Nation-State in Africa*, Uppsala: Nordic African Institute

Williams, E., 1945, *Capitalism or Slavery*, London: Longman

Wilson, A., 1989, *US Foreign Policy and Revolution: The Creation of Tanzania*, London: Pluto

Yieke, F. A., ed. 2005, *East Africa: In Search of National and Regional Renewal*, Dakar: CODESRIA

 SILENCES IN NGO DISCOURSE

Notes

1 This paper was originally given as the keynote paper to the Symposium on NGOs in Arusha, Tanzania in November 2005.

2 Press Release, US Embassy in Tanzania, 29 July, 2003.

3 The irony of Blair's Africa Commission turns cynical when it is recalled that one of Blair's commissioners, President Mkapa, comes from the same country whose first President, Nyerere, in retirement, chaired the South Commission which was conceived and financed by the South!

REFLECTIONS ON NGOS IN TANZANIA: WHAT WE ARE, WHAT WE ARE NOT AND WHAT WE OUGHT TO BE[1]

Soul-searching

We do not get many opportunities to sit back and reflect on ourselves as civil society activists. Reflecting on who we are, what are we doing and where we are going does not require any justification. In this age of imperial hegemony, transmitted to the peoples of the world through both state and non-state agencies, it is all the more important that we create opportunities and consciously ask ourselves fundamental questions: Are we serving the best interests of our working people? Are we contributing to the great cause of humanity, the cause of emancipation from oppression, exploitation and deprivation? Or are we engaged, consciously or unconsciously, in playing to the tune set by others?

It is in this spirit of self-criticism, reflection and soul-searching that I want to offer a few thoughts, which I hope we can discuss honestly.

Our limitations

To understand NGOs better, we must start by asking what we are, what we are not, and what our limitations are. Firstly, most of our NGOs are top–down organisations led by the elite. What is more, most of them are urban based. In our case, NGOs did not begin as a response to the expressed need of the large majority of working people. It is true that many of us working in the NGOs are well intentioned. We want to contribute to some cause, however we may define it. It is also true that some NGOs do address some of the real concerns of the working people.

Yet, we must recognise that we did not develop as, nor have we managed to become, organic to the mass of the people, at least so far. The relationship between the NGOs and the masses therefore remains, at best, that of benefactors and beneficiaries. This is not the best of relationships when it comes to genuine activism with, rather than for, the people.

Secondly, we are not constituency or membership based organisations. Even if we have a membership, this largely constitutes fellow members of the elite. Our accountability therefore is limited, and limited to a small group of people. In fact, we may end up being more accountable to the donors who fund us than to our members, let alone our people.

Thirdly, we are funded by and rely almost exclusively on foreign funding. This is the greatest single limitation. 'He who pays the piper calls the tune' holds true, however much we may wish to think otherwise. In many direct and subtle ways, those who fund us determine our agenda, or place limits on or reorient them. Very few of us can really resist the pressures that external funding imposes on us.

In the NGO-world we have been brought up to believe that we should act and not theorise. Theorisation is detested. The result is that most 'NGO-wallahs' do not have any grand vision of society. Nor are they guided by large issues. Rather they concentrate on small, day-to-day matters. In the NGOs, we hardly spend any time defining our vision in relation to the overall social and economic context of our societies.

Many of us tend to conflate NGOs with civil society organisations thus undermining the traditional member and class-based organisations of the working people, such as trade unions and peasant associations. We may pay lip-service to people's organisations, but in practice, both our benefactors – the so-called donor community – and we ourselves privilege NGOs. This has had far-reaching consequences, including even to undermine the people's organisations themselves.

In spite of these limitations, I do believe that NGOs can play some worthy role. But we do have to recognise what we are not. I want to suggest that in the current context of neoliberal imperialist hegemony, NGOs have been cast in a surrogate role in our country, which many of us have come to accept. We may even feel flattered. This is where our limitations have been compounded. There is a danger that we assume a role which does not belong to us, and fail to play the role for which we may best be suited. This will become clearer as I examine some of our recent experiences of activism.

Participation by substitution

NGOs, as they developed in the West, were essentially pressure groups to keep those in power, the state and the government, on their toes. In our case, as donors became disenchanted with states, they took a fancy to NGOs, thus undermining the state and its institutions while at the same time placating their own domestic constituencies demanding civil society involvement.

Participation and consultation are supposedly part of 'good governance', insisted on by donors, and allowing the

---

'Africa must refuse to be humiliated, exploited, and pushed around. And with the same determination we must refuse to humiliate, exploit, or push others around.'

---

imperial countries to legitimise the neoliberal policies of dominant Western powers and the international financial institutions (IFIs) in our countries.

NGOs are cast in the role of 'partners': partners of the state, partners of the erstwhile donor community, partners in development, and partners in good governance. We get involved in so-called policy dialogues in which the triad of NGOs, government and donor representatives participate. We attend workshops as stakeholders. Donors who fund policy-making and their consultants who make policies seek us out for consultation. All this passes for people's participation and involvement, or what is called 'good governance'. But what is the implication of this type of participation for democratic governance in our countries?

One of the core functions and responsibilities of a government is policy making in the interest of its people. It is emphatically not the function of donors. Donor-driven policy making simply shows how much our states and people have lost the right to self-determination under the imperialist domination of the post-Cold War period, euphemistically called globalisation.

By participating in this process NGOs lend legitimacy to this domination. In fact the NGOs ought to be playing exactly the opposite role. NGOs cannot possibly be fighting in the interest of the people if they are not in a position to expose and oppose imperial domination. The right to self-determination is our basic right as a people, as a nation, as a country. It is the right for which our independence fighters laid down their lives. Now we seem to be legitimising the process of losing it.

By pretending to be partners in policy making, NGOs let the government off the hook as the government abdicates its primary responsibility. The role of NGOs ought to be that of watchdog, critiquing shortcomings in government policies and their implementation.

NGOs cannot simply substitute themselves for the people. They are neither the elected representatives of the people nor mandated to represent them. Participation in the institutions of state is the democratic right of all peoples. It ought to be done on a continuous basis through structuring of appropriate legal, institutional and social frameworks.

As pressure and advocacy groups, our primary duty as NGOs is to pressurise the powers-that-be to create conditions that enable participation of the people themselves in the institutions of policy making. This means our role should be to struggle for the expansion of space for the people and people's organisations in the representative institutions of the state such as parliament, local government councils, and village and neighbourhood bodies.

The process of reforming and reconstituting the state in a democratic direction is the only way to ensure genuine popular participation, and to deter abuse of state power. This is a continuous process of struggle, and cannot be reduced to some one-off ad hoc process of stakeholder workshops and policy dialogues.

If the struggle for democratic reform were thus conceived, then the strategy itself of the NGOs would change. There would be protracted public debates instead of stakeholder conferences, the development of alternative ways of doing things instead of so-called inputs into consultants' policy drafts. There would be demonstrations, protest marches and teach-ins in streets and community centres to expose serious abuses of power and bad polices, instead of the so-called policy dialogues in five-star hotels. Democratic governance would be an arena where power is contested, not some moral dialogue or crusade for goodness against evil, as the meaningless term 'good governance' implies. You cannot dialogue with power.

In short, I am urging that we need to re-examine our conceptualisation and practice of the new and fancy roles of partners and stakeholders we are being given. We cannot possibly be partners and hold a stake in a system that oppresses and dehumanises the large majority of people.

Selective activism

The great strength of the NGOs is supposed to be their consistent, principled and committed stand for human values

---

As long as the NGOs participate in stakeholder workshops, discussing poverty alleviation strategy papers, they seem to be oblivious to the creation of poverty through redundancy and the robbery of public goods as social services are privatised.

---

and causes in the interest of the popular masses. We are not a bunch of self-seeking petty bourgeois politicians, who are inconsistent almost by definition, driven more by power than principles. We activists are not in the business of brokering power where expediency and compromise rule. Our business is to resist and expose the ugly face of power. We are guided and our work is informed by deeply held human values and causes. It seems to me that consistency of principles and commitment to humanity should inform all our work, thought, activism and advocacy.

Our values and causes may be summed as three elements, which I have elsewhere called popular livelihoods, popular participation and popular power.[2] Whether expressed in the language of democracy or human rights, most of our values and causes can be summed up in these

SILENCES IN NGO DISCOURSE

three elements. By 'popular' I mean to refer to the exploited and oppressed classes and groups in our society. This is
in contrast to the current, utterly demeaning and singularly
useless, neoliberal discourse in which popular classes are
dubbed the 'poor', to be incessantly researched upon, and
targeted to receive poverty alleviation funds.

The term 'popular' is meant to signify the central place
of the working people in the struggle to regain their livelihoods, dignity and power. I shall not go into details of these
concepts here. Suffice to say that I believe these elements
signify the values and causes with which many NGOs
and activists identify. It is my contention that many of our
NGOs have failed to stand up for these values consistently,
and have thereby greatly compromised themselves. Let me
cite three recent experiences. I am doing this as a matter of
critical reflection rather than to point fingers.

In 2003 the whole world was shaken to the core and basic
human values were cynically challenged when the United
States invaded and occupied Iraq. Millions of people all
over the world demonstrated and protested in great defi-
ance of this monstrosity – as individuals, as NGO activists,
as simple decent human beings. Here in Dar es Salaam, our
NGO world was shamefully silent. A small demonstration
organised by the university student union attracted a few
NGOs and activists. But well-known human rights NGOs
and advocates were conspicuous in their absence. The
umbrella NGO organisations did not so much as issue a
simple statement, either on their own or in solidarity with
others. How can we who espouse democratic values of
freedom and self-determination explain such silence?

Let us take the second example. During the time that

60

our government was debating the NGO bill, one of the most draconian bills, the so-called 'anti-terrorism law', was being discussed. The NGO bill was rightly opposed by NGOs. One may critique their strategy. That is another matter for another occasion. The point here is that these same NGOs were utterly silent on the anti-terrorism bill. In South Africa and Kenya, NGOs were in the forefront against the anti-terrorism law. To their credit, our sister NGOs in Kenya have put up such stiff resistance that the bill has not yet been passed. But ours sailed through parliament. Many people are asking and are entitled to ask: how come? Are we NGOs selective in the freedoms we support? Was our cowardly silence in respect of the anti-terrorism law because our benefactors include the likes of USAID? Is it because we are just like any other self-seeking group in that we readily challenged the NGO bill that threatened our own existence, while conveniently ignoring the anti-terrorism law, which delivers a shattering blow to all basic freedoms and rights?

It is true that NGOs cannot do everything and be everywhere. But the question of Iraq and the spate of anti-terrorism laws and measures thrust down the throats of our government and people is not just anything. It marks an important turning point in the establishment of imperial hegemony of the single superpower with far-reaching consequences for the freedoms, rights, dignity and independence of the peoples of the world, particularly the Third World.

Under the pretext of fighting terrorism, the superpower is involved in changing the world map. It is playing god by deciding for us what is good and what is evil. It is establishing a string of training colleges for spies and new types of police on the continent, including in our own country. Yet, the NGO world sleeps soundly. Latin America knows, and has experienced, what happens when you have your forces of 'law and order' trained in methods of disappearances, mysterious murders and preemptive killings of those labelled 'terrorists'. A whole people – those we used to call freedom fighters, liberators and organic intellectuals of the people – become non-people! Witness the atrocities suffered by Central and Latin America, from El Salvador to Nicaragua, from Argentina to Chile. Many perpetrators of these horrendous crimes were 'trained' in the so-called School of the Americas sponsored by the notorious CIA. Surely, no NGO worth its salt can ignore the lessons from other continents and stand on the sidelines whilst the seeds of instability are planted on our continent?

Solidarity with people's organisations

In the 1980s and 1990s, many activists enthusiastically struggled for the opening of organisational space for the people. That was when NGOs mushroomed, and the multi-party system was introduced. Coming out of the background of the domination of the authoritarian state, which killed and maimed people's independent organisational initiatives, it is quite understandable that we were in the forefront of the struggle for the independence of civil society. Yet, in the larger context of the moral and ideological rehabilitation of imperialism in the post-Cold War era, NGOs appear to have undermined traditional people's organisations, just as human rights ideology has displaced ideologies of national liberation and social emancipation.

Many NGOs have failed to realise this. Therefore they may be lending credence to this process, without being necessarily conscious of it.

As a third example, let us look at trade unions in our country. The trade union movement was first suppressed in 1964, before political parties in 1965. Freedom to form political parties was reintroduced in 1992; freedom to

---

The question facing us is: Can we really better understand the existing world so as to create a better world without a grand vision, a grand theory, a worldview rooted in the experiences of the working people? Can we really eschew thinking, theorising and knowing?

---

form trade unions came only in 1998. Since then, against very strong odds and under adverse conditions, the trade unions have been struggling to establish themselves as truly class and constituency-based organisations.

Privatisation and globalisation have greatly undermined the efforts of the working class. It is being decimated through redundancy, and impoverished as public social services such as water, sanitation, education, electricity and health are turned into private commodities for sale on the market in the interest of private profit.

Nonetheless, the fledging trade unions have been

63

SILENCES IN NGO DISCOURSE

involved in a desperate struggle against the new exploit-
ers, the so-called *wawekezaji*. This includes South African
capital, which is moving north ferociously in its second
round of primitive accumulation on the continent. We have
witnessed the saga of the workers of the National Bank of
Commerce (NBC). What is interesting and inexplicable is
that the NGOs played no role at all in these struggles, not
even expressing solidarity.

As long as the NGOs participate in stakeholder workshops, discussing poverty alleviation strategy papers, they
seem to be oblivious to the creation of poverty through
redundancy and the robbery of public goods as social services are privatised. When the NBC workers were holding
their mass meetings, sister trade unions sent delegations to
express solidarity. I did not see or hear of any NGO doing
the same.

A lack of understanding amongst the NGOs of our correct place and role in the struggles of the working people
manifests itself on other levels. There have been massive
anti-globalisation and anti-capitalist movements in the
West. But again, our presence there is not very prominent.
In our own situation, the Lawyers Environmental Action
Team (LEAT)[3] has been involved in a protracted exposure
of the abuses of the mining companies. But our NGOs and
their umbrella organisations have remained quiet. We have
not uttered even a word of solidarity, let alone held demonstrations and protests in militant solidarity.

64

Conclusion: Articulating an activist world view and choosing sides

I want to suggest that we, the NGOs and activists, need to look at ourselves hard. We must take stock of our activities. We must evaluate ourselves in the light of our values, principles and mission to create a better world. If an alternative world is indeed possible – and it is – we need to know our existing world. Not only know the existing world, but also know who is running it. Why and how does the existing world keep reproducing itself? In whose interest? For what purpose? And we have to choose sides: the side of those who are struggling for a better world against those who want to maintain the existing world. Put simply, we cannot be neutral.

The question facing us is: Can we really better understand the existing world so as to create a better world without a grand vision, a grand theory, a worldview rooted in the experiences of the working people? Can we really eschew thinking, theorising and knowing? The dominant powers and their spokespersons speak of the 'end of history' and the 'end of ideology'. They tell us the age of solidarity with the oppressed peoples is gone. We are told: now is the age of economics, not politics.

Our leaders tell us there is only one world: the existing world, the globalised world, the hegemonic world. 'Either sink or swim', they say. The truth of the matter is that the working people are sinking in the globalised world, while the elite are swimming in it. It is clear therefore that there is a contest between two worldviews: one which wants to maintain the existing world; the other that wants to cre-

ate an alternative world. Which worldview do we share? We must make a choice, and act in accordance with our choice.

Let me end with two very poignant quotations broadly representing the two worldviews in a specific context. A story in *The Guardian* reporting on the new Tanzanian foreign policy claimed it stressed economic interests rather than political considerations. At the end of the story the US ambassador, speaking to the Parliamentary Committee for Foreign Affairs on 29 July 2003, is quoted. Commending Tanzania for its new 'economic diplomacy', he says:

> The liberation diplomacy of the past, when alliances with socialist nations were paramount and so-called Third World solidarity dominated foreign policy, must give way to a more realistic approach to dealing with your true friends – those who are working to lift you into the 21st century where poverty is not acceptable and disease must be conquered.

Some 30 years ago former independence leader and president of Tanzania Mwalimu Nyerere, commenting about the need to change another 'realistic' world – apartheid South Africa – said:

> Humanity has already passed through many phases since man began his evolutionary journey. And nature shows us that not all life evolves in the same way. The chimpanzees – to whom once we were very near – got on to the wrong evolutionary path and they got stuck. And there were other species which

became extinct; their teeth were so big, or their bodies so heavy, that they could not adapt to changing circumstances and they died out.

I am convinced that, in the history of the human race, imperialists and racialists will also become extinct. They are now very powerful. But they are a very primitive animal. The only difference between them and these other extinct creatures is that their teeth and claws are more elaborate and cause much greater harm...

But failure to co-operate together is a mark of bestiality; it is not a characteristic of humanity. Imperialists and racialists will go. Vorster, and all like him, will come to an end. Every racialist in the world is an animal of some kind or the other, and all are kinds that have no future. Eventually they will become extinct. Africa must refuse to be humiliated, exploited, and pushed around. And with the same determination we must refuse to humiliate, exploit, or push others around. We must act, not just say words.[4]

The pundits of the status quo have in common with all dominating classes and hegemonic powers the assumption that the existing world is the only realistic world, and no alternative world is possible. Yet, it is the struggle for an alternative world, a better world, which has changed the past and will continue to change the present for a better future. We, the activists, together with the working people, must continue to fight for a better world. An alternative world is possible.

SILENCES IN NGO DISCOURSE

Notes

1 This paper was originally given as a keynote address to the Gender Festival organised by the Tanzania Gender Networking Group in September 2003. I am grateful to Natasha Shivji for reading and commenting on the draft.

2 See Issa Shivji, 2000, 'Critical Elements of a New Democratic Consensus in Africa' in Othman, H. (ed.) *Reflections on Leadership in Africa: Forty Years after Independence*, Belgium: VUB Brussels University Press.

3 See <www.leat.or.tz>.

4 Julius Nyerere, 1973, *Freedom and Development: A Selection from Writings and Speeches*, Oxford University Press, p. 371.

CPSIA information can be obtained at www.ICGtesting.com
Printed in the USA
BVOW011946080113

310120BV00007B/121/A